DiscoverRoo
An Imprint of Pop!
popbooksonline.com

World Religions

BUDDHISM

by Elizabeth Andrews

WELCOME TO DiscoverRoo!

This book is filled with videos, puzzles, games, and more! Scan the QR codes* while you read, or visit the website below to make this book pop.

popbooksonline.com/buddhism

abdobooks.com

Published by Pop!, a division of ABDO, PO Box 398166, Minneapolis, Minnesota 55439.

Printed in China.

052023
082023

Cover Photo: Shutterstock Images
Interior Photos: Shutterstock Images
Editor: Tyler Gieseke
Series Designer: Laura Graphenteen

Library of Congress Control Number: 2022950553

Publisher's Cataloging-in-Publication Data

Names: Andrews, Elizabeth, author.
Title: Buddhism / by Elizabeth Andrews
Description: Minneapolis, Minnesota : Pop!, 2024 | Series: World religions | Includes online resources and index
Identifiers: ISBN 9781098244439 (lib. bdg.) | ISBN 9781098245139 (ebook)
Subjects: LCSH: Buddhism--Doctrines--History--Juvenile literature. | Buddhism and culture--Juvenile literature. | World religions--Juvenile literature. | Religious belief--Juvenile literature.
Classification: DDC 294.3--dc23

*Scanning QR codes requires a web-enabled smart device with a QR code reader app and a camera.

TABLE OF CONTENTS

CHAPTER 1

BUDDHA'S BEGINNING

People follow different religions across the world. A religion is an organized practice of faith and **worship**. There are more than 10,000 religions in the world. Buddhism is followed by seven percent of the world. Most Buddhists live in Asia.

WATCH A VIDEO HERE!

Buddhists sprinkle water on statues of the Buddha in the spring to cleanse their souls.

It was predicted at Siddhartha's birth that he would change the world.

Buddhism was started around 500 BCE by Siddhartha Gautama. He was a prince. He lived a comfortable life protected by his father, the king, in a palace. But Siddhartha wanted to understand life outside. So, he left his home and family for the first time.

Beyond the palace, Siddhartha saw sickness, aging, and death for the first time. He learned that life is suffering and everyone dies. Siddhartha also saw a man meditating under a tree. He felt like that was his future.

Siddhartha Gautama was born fully formed with his hair in a bun. He could walk right away.

Siddhartha left his family and possessions. He wanted to free himself and others from all pain and suffering. Siddhartha went on a **spiritual** journey. He met teachers, slept in the forest, begged for food, and meditated. He wanted to overcome his human needs and break the cycle of death and rebirth.

Siddhartha meditated for 49 days beneath a bodhi tree. He had to fight off demons during it. The demons did not like what he was learning during meditation.

Siddhartha beat the demons. During the meditation Siddhartha became enlightened. This means he learned to free himself from the cycle of pain and suffering. This realization turned Siddhartha into the Buddha. While alive, the Buddha taught others how to overcome their pain and suffering.

The Buddha first taught his old spiritual teachers what he learned.

CHAPTER 2

REACHING NIRVANA

Buddhists believe they are part of a big **universe** with many worlds besides Earth. When a being dies, it will be born again into something different. The cycle of death and rebirth is called samsara. The Buddha discovered ways to free people from the cycle.

LEARN MORE HERE!

Buddhist art often shows images that represent cycles.

DID YOU KNOW?

Ghosts are the worst thing to be reborn as. They cannot be seen and are trapped, hungry, and unable to eat anything.

Buddhists believe in the Three Jewels. They are the *Buddha*, the *dharma*, and the *sangha*. Dharma means the teaching of the Four Noble Truths. The first truth is that life is suffering. The second is that suffering is caused by **desires**. The third is that one can be free of desires. This freedom is called nirvana. The Buddha reached nirvana when he became

The sleeping Buddha represents his final moments on Earth.

enlightened. The fourth Noble Truth is the Eightfold Path to nirvana.

Nirvana is a state beyond existence. This state is difficult to understand. Luckily, it doesn't need to be understood to work toward it. Reaching nirvana is the goal of Buddhists. The Buddha taught that the Eightfold Path will help people reach nirvana.

Part of the path involves meditation. Meditation helps quiet and transform the mind. It encourages Buddhists to concentrate on their attachment to suffering and desire. One way to meditate is to notice what is in your mind without reacting to it.

KARMA

Karma carries the effects of a person's actions, good or bad. Good karma means a person may be reborn as a god or royalty. Bad karma means a person might come back as a street rat or ghost. People can make good choices in their current lives to build up karma for their rebirth.

Following the Eightfold Path helps a person live a balanced life. Anyone can be released from their suffering and reach nirvana like the Buddha. In fact, the Buddha was just a regular person when he started his own journey.

THE EIGHTFOLD PATH

RIGHT VIEW
know the truth

RIGHT INTENTION
free your mind of evil

RIGHT SPEECH
say nothing that hurts others

RIGHT ACTION
work for the good of others

RIGHT LIVELIHOOD
respect life

RIGHT EFFORT
resist evil

RIGHT CONCENTRATION
practice meditation

RIGHT MINDFULNESS
control your thoughts

KEY

WISDOM These steps help a person accept the Four Noble Truths and live by them.

MORALITY These steps are about doing. A person should live correctly by causing no harm to others through their speech or actions. They should also protect nature.

PERSONAL THOUGHTS These steps can be followed with meditation. One should focus on keeping a positive attitude. The goal is to release desires and stop suffering.

CHAPTER 3

BUDDHIST TEACHERS

The third Jewel of Buddhism is the sangha. It is the **spiritual** community of Buddhist monks, nuns, and others who encourage spiritual growth in Buddhism. Monks and nuns teach and lead people along the path to nirvana.

EXPLORE LINKS HERE!

Buddhist altars can have large or small statues of the Buddha.

Donating to monks and monasteries is called daña.

Monks and nuns are Buddhists who live away from society. Their lives revolve around the Eightfold Path. The first monks and nuns wore simple robes, slept outside, and ate only what others gave them. Later, they formed permanent communities together called monasteries. Monasteries are often in the forest or mountains.

Today, monks and nuns still live with very little. They follow rules such as not lying or stealing. During the day, monks and nuns walk through the local villages for food donations. They also do chores in the monastery, meditate, meet with their own teachers, and study Buddhist readings.

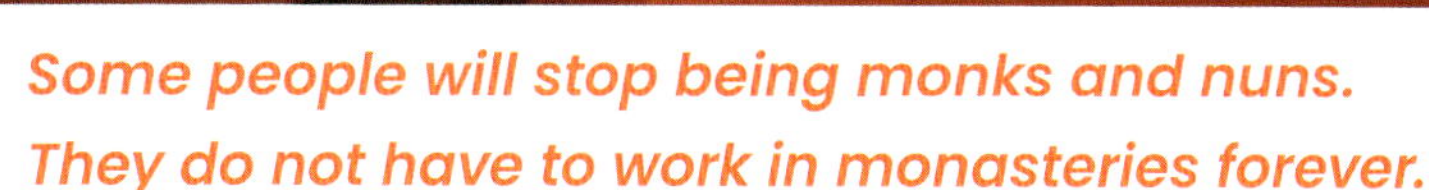

Some people will stop being monks and nuns. They do not have to work in monasteries forever.

少林寺

In China, there is a temple that trains warrior monks. They learn kung fu along with their meditation and Buddhist readings.

The sangha serves the Buddhist community by connecting the old traditions with **modern**-day people. Monks and nuns teach about the Eightfold Path because they understand it deeply and practice it daily.

Monks who learn kung fu often focus on strengthening their bodies and their minds equally.

CHAPTER 4

LAY BUDDHISTS

Lay Buddhists are people who follow the religion but are not monks or nuns. They work to connect with the Buddha and receive the dharma. Buddhists **devote** themselves to Buddha's teachings in different ways. Meditating is an important practice for all Buddhists.

COMPLETE AN ACTIVITY HERE!

DID YOU KNOW?

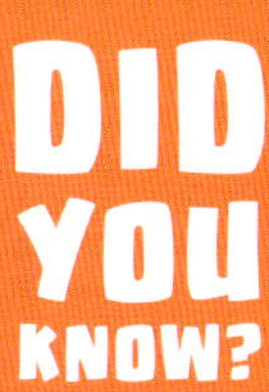

The self is an idea created in the mind. It is not real. Buddha teaches that a person is not an individual. A person is only part of a soul's large cycle.

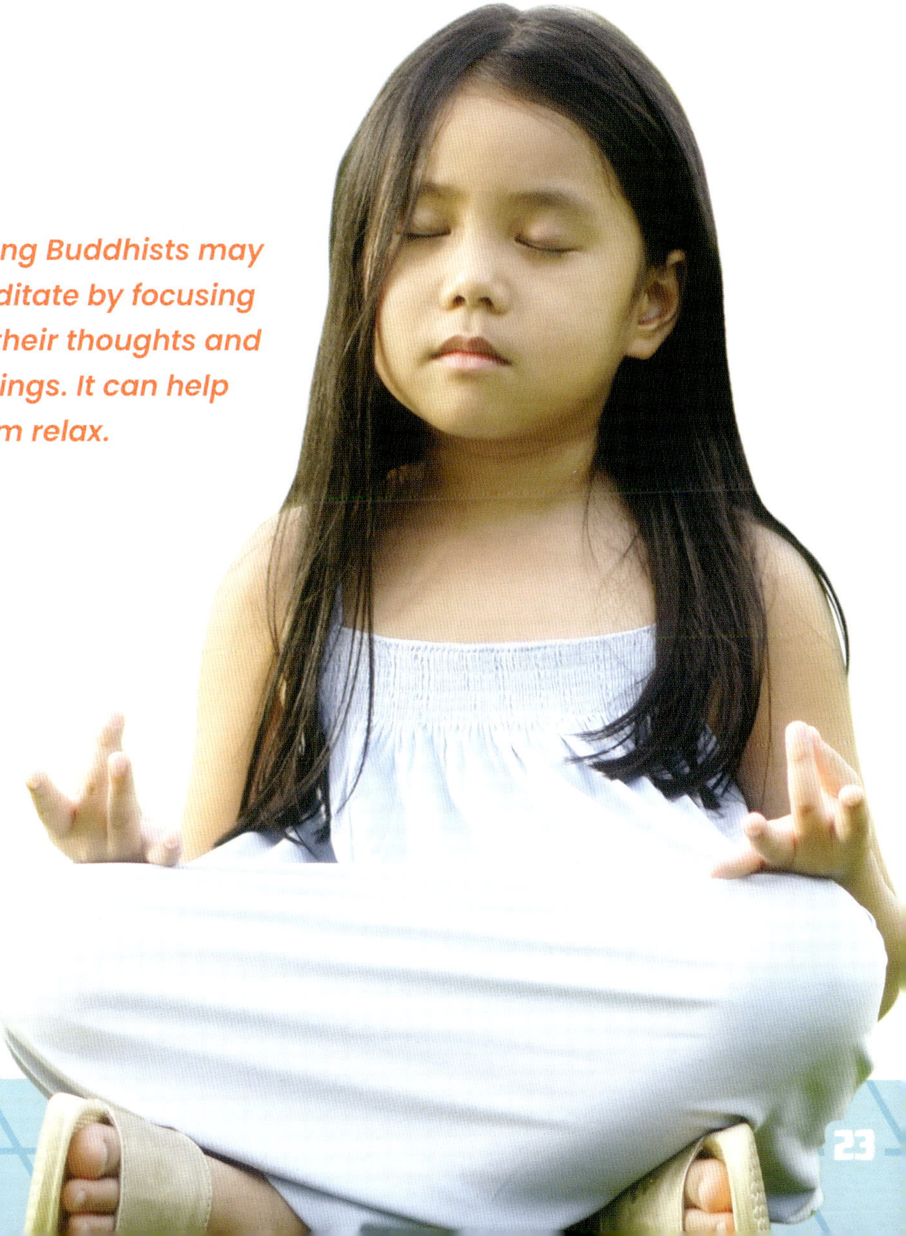

Young Buddhists may meditate by focusing on their thoughts and feelings. It can help them relax.

Buddhist temples are beautiful. They can be very colorful or even covered in gold!

Laypeople will visit temples. There they pray and bow before **altars**. They may make offerings like fruit and flowers. Some Buddhists will watch monks and nuns perform **rituals**. These actions help a person along the Eightfold Path. Lay Buddhists also make food or money donations to monasteries. This creates good karma for a person's next life.

Stupas are buildings that contain a **relic** of the Buddha or religious book. People walk clockwise around the stupa to show their devotion.

People don't wear shoes in a Buddhist temple. Bringing in any dirt is disrespectful.

Bathing statues of the Buddha symbolizes the bath he was given on the day he was born.

Buddhists celebrate several holidays. They have their own New Year. There is a special day when lay Buddhists bring clothes, bedding, and other daily necessities to monasteries. The most important celebration is Wesak. It is the Buddha's birthday! Buddhists decorate temples with flowers and banners. They wash statues of the Buddha to cleanse their hearts.

A seated Buddha with his right hand up and facing outward symbolizes protection and overcoming fear.

Monks may speak with visitors and answer questions about Buddhism.

Millions of people all over the world practice Buddhism. Followers are learning how to be balanced and free from suffering. The religion is filled with beautiful leaders, temples, and individuality. It is a complex religion that adds color to the great big world.

Lotus flowers grow in muddy water. Buddhists believe the mud represents the struggle of life and the beautiful bloom symbolizes Buddha's teachings.

MAKING CONNECTIONS

TEXT-TO-SELF

What part of Buddhism are you most curious about? Please explain your answer.

TEXT-TO-TEXT

Have you ready any books about different religions? How are those religions similar to or different from Buddhism?

TEXT-TO-WORLD

Times have changed since Buddha was alive. Do you think it has become easier or more difficult for Buddhists to let go of their troubles and desires? Please explain your answer.

GLOSSARY

altar — a raised table or platform used for religious purposes.

desire — something one wants or wishes for.

devotion — strong affection, respect, and dedication.

modern — having to do with the present or current time.

relic — something that has survived from the past. Buddhist relics include the ashes of Buddha's remains.

ritual — a set of actions always done in the same way, often because of tradition.

spiritual — having to do with religious matters or people's beliefs in things such as the soul or what happens after death.

symbolize — to serve as a symbol. A symbol is an object or mark that stands for an idea.

universe — all existing things including the Earth and heavens.

worship — love, respect, and affection shown to an object, person, or being.

INDEX

DiscoverRoo!
ONLINE RESOURCES

This book is filled with videos, puzzles, games, and more! Scan the QR codes* while you read, or visit the website below to make this book pop.

popbooksonline.com/buddhism

*Scanning QR codes requires a web-enabled smart device with a QR code reader app and a camera.